We live on a planet called Earth.

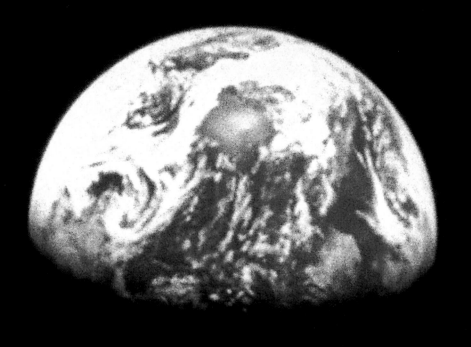

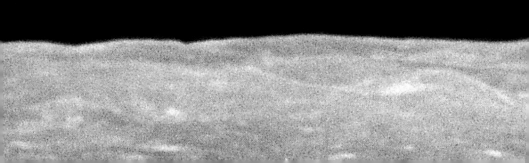

Earth is one of eight planets
that travel around the sun.
The sun and everything
that travels around it
are called the solar system.

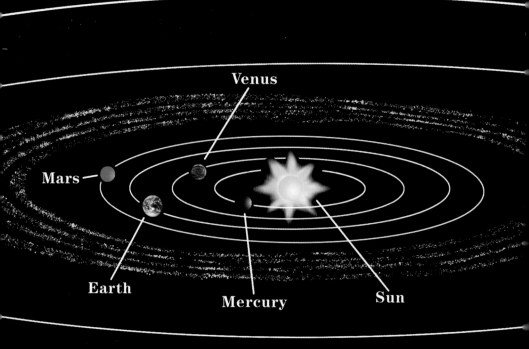

Venus

Mars

Earth

Mercury

Sun

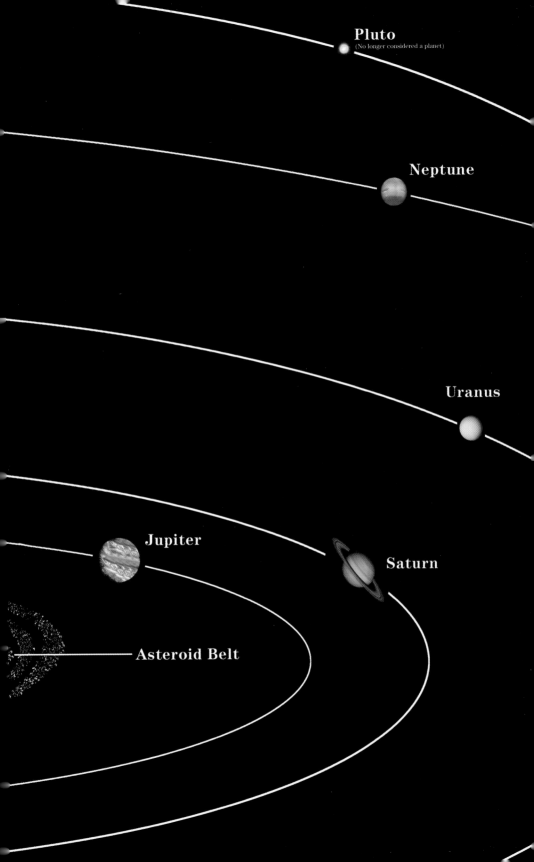

Pluto
(No longer considered a planet)

Neptune

Uranus

Jupiter

Saturn

Asteroid Belt

The sun is a giant ball

of fiery hot gases.

If Earth were the size

of a basketball,

the sun would be as big

as a basketball court.

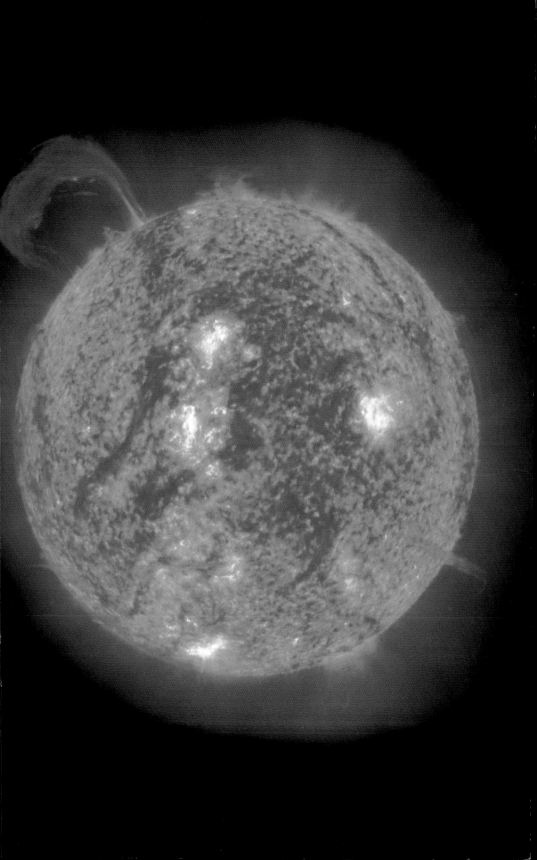

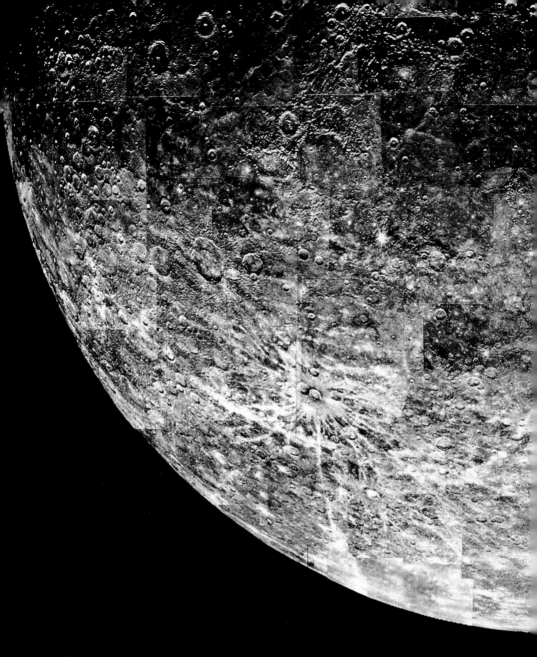

Mercury is closest to the sun.

During the day, its temperature

is almost 800 degrees.

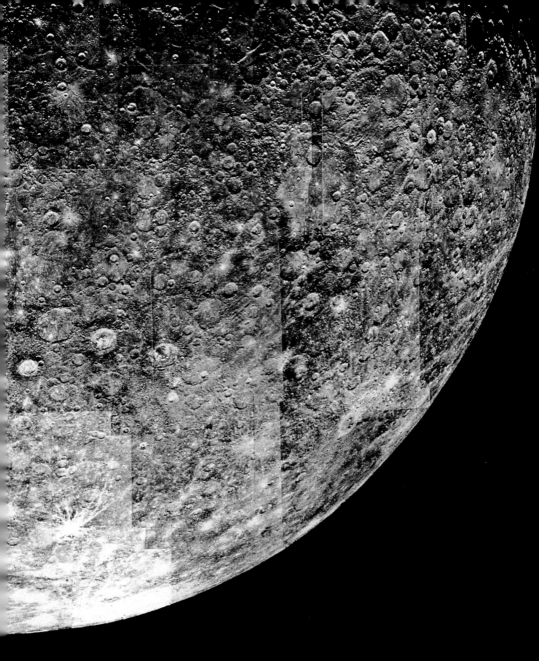

But at night, the temperature drops to nearly 300 degrees below zero.

Venus is about the same size
as Earth, but it is very different.
Thick clouds cover the planet
but it has no water.
Venus is the hottest planet
in our solar system.

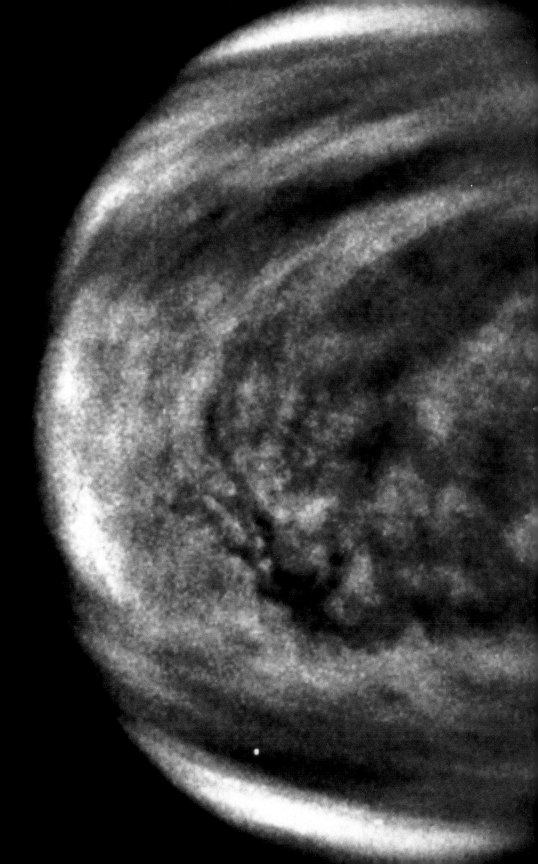

Earth is the only planet
that has water on its surface.

If Earth were closer to the sun,
the oceans would boil away.
If it were farther away,
the oceans would freeze.

Earth's moon is not a planet.

Planets travel around the sun.

Moons travel around planets.

Even though Earth's moon

is 250,000 miles away,

it is our closest neighbor.

**Phases
of the
Moon**

new moon

crescent moon

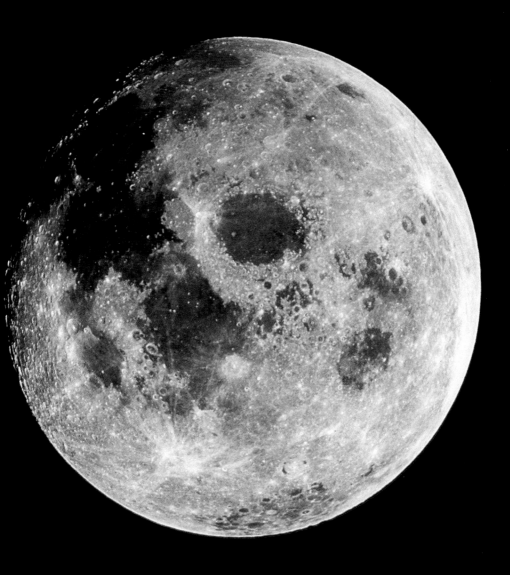

quarter moon

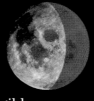

gibbous moon

full moon

The surface of Mars is
a red, dusty soil.
Spacecraft from Earth
have landed on Mars.

People are interested in looking for signs of life there. But so far they have found no signs of life.

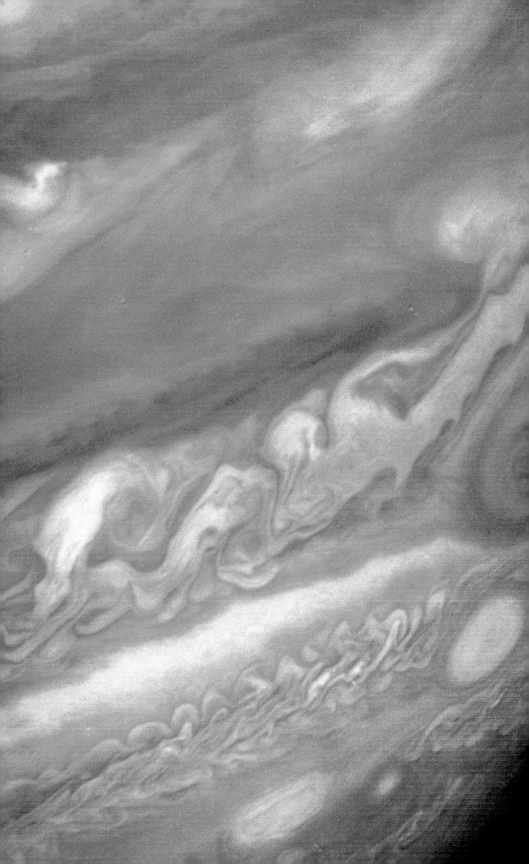

Jupiter is much larger
than all of the other planets
combined.
The surface of Jupiter is
an ocean of liquid hydrogen
10,000 miles deep.
The Great Red Spot is
a giant storm on Jupiter.
This storm is bigger
than Earth.

Saturn is the second largest planet.

Saturn has rings made

of pieces of ice, rock, and dust.

Some pieces are smaller

than a dime.

Others are as big as a house.

Uranus is a green planet. Its very thin rings are made of an unknown black material. Uranus has 5 large moons and at least 16 smaller ones.

Neptune is a blue-green
planet with giant storms
on its surface.
Freezing winds blow
across Neptune
at speeds of up to
700 miles per hour.

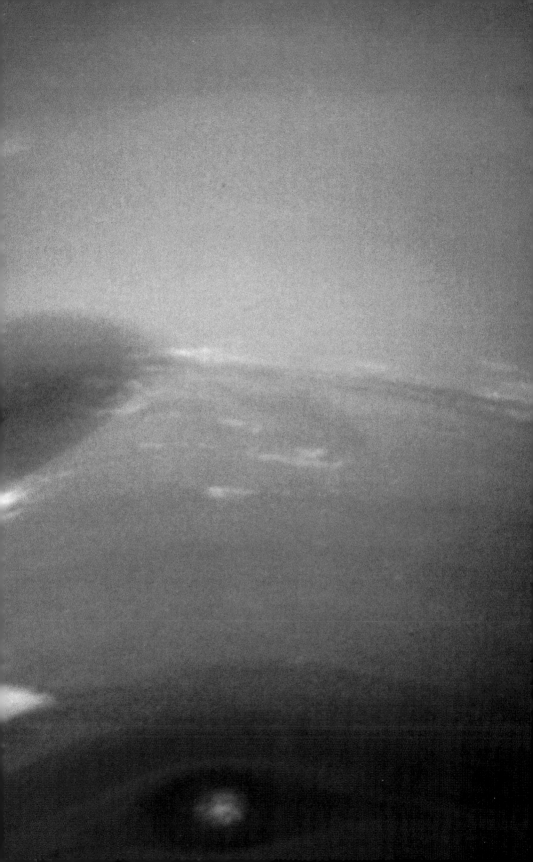

Pluto is a distant ball of mostly frozen gases. For many years, Pluto was called the ninth planet in our solar system. In 2006, scientists decided that Pluto should not be called a planet because it was not big enough. They now call Pluto a dwarf planet along with the asteroid Ceres and another distant icy object called Xena.

Asteroids are
chunks of rock.
They are much
smaller than planets.
About 4,000 asteroids
circle the sun between
Mars and Jupiter.
This area is called
the asteroid belt.

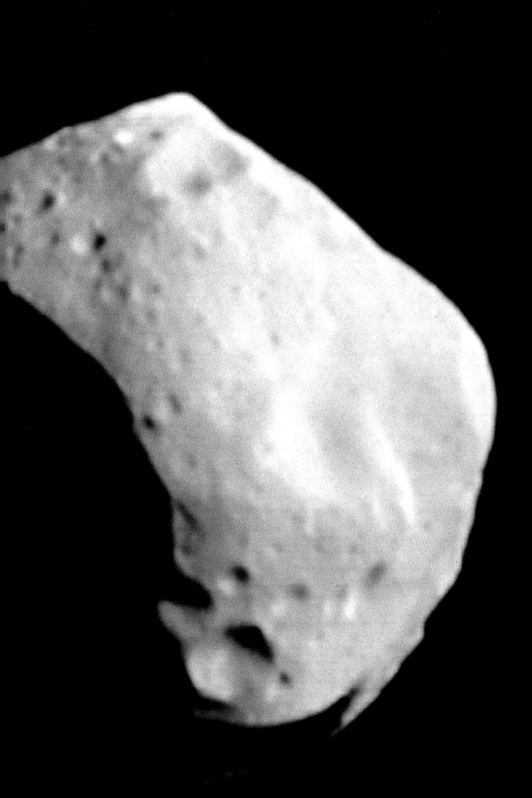

Far out in space, other planets

circle other stars.

But no one knows if any

distant planets are like Earth.

We still have much to learn

about planets and stars.

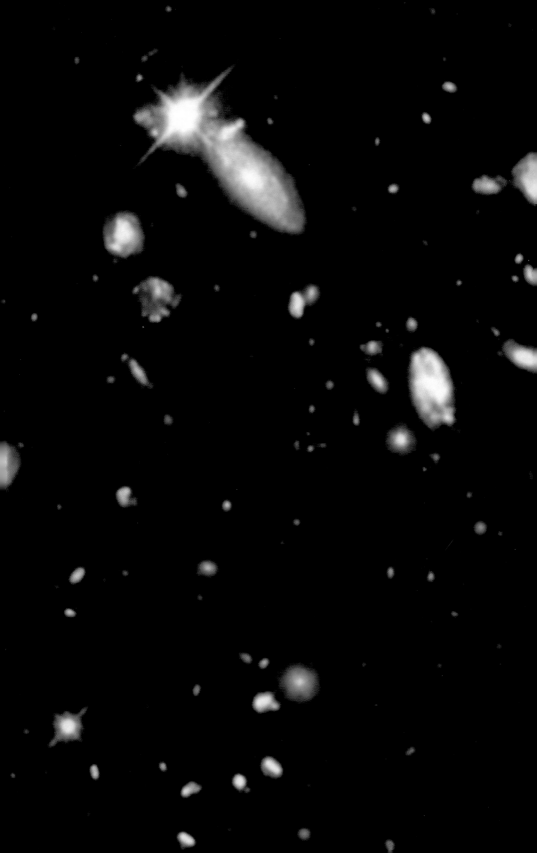

	Mercury	Venus	Earth	Mars	Jupiter	Saturn	Uranus	Neptune	Pluto (No longer considered a planet)
Distance from Sun (millions of miles)	36	67	93	142	484	891	1785	2793	3647
Orbital Period (days)	88	225	365	687	4331	10,747	30,589	59,800	90,588
Diameter (miles)	3032	7521	7926	4222	88,846	74,897	31,763	30,775	1485
Length of Day (hours)	4223	2802	24	25	10	11	17	16	153
Average Temperature (F)	333	867	59	-85	-166	-220	-320	-330	-375
Moons	0	0	1	2	28	30	21	8	1
Rings	No	No	No	No	Yes	Yes	Yes	Yes	No